Franklin and Eleanor Roosevelt

THEIR

ESSENTIAL

WISDOM

EDITED BY
CAROL KELLY-GANGI

New York

To Dad with love and gratitude—
for teaching me at an early age
the wonder and value of history.

FALL RIVER PRESS

New York

An Imprint of Sterling Publishing
387 Park Avenue South
New York, NY 10016

Book design by Rich Hazelton
Jacket design by David Ter-Avanesyan

All images courtesy of Library of Congress

ISBN 978-1-4351-5569-5

For information about custom editions, special sales, and premium and
corporate purchases, please contact Sterling Special Sales at 800-805-5489
or specialsales@sterlingpublishing.com.

Manufactured in the United States of America

2 4 6 8 10 9 7 5 3 1

www.sterlingpublishing.com

CONTENTS

Contents

INTRODUCTION

On August 13, 1921, Franklin Delano Roosevelt lay immobilized in his bed, completely paralyzed from the chest down. Just days before, he'd been enjoying the summer with his family and some close friends at their Campobello retreat. After a day spent swimming with his children, he felt weak and listless; he skipped dinner and went upstairs to bed. Within a day, he lost the ability to walk and all feeling in his legs. Within weeks, doctors confirmed the grim diagnosis of polio.

By March of the following year, Franklin was fitted with heavy steel leg braces. The only way he would ever walk again was with the use of braces and crutches. Franklin's mother, Sara, a loving but controlling woman, implored him to return to Hyde Park and live a quiet life as an invalid. Franklin and his wife, Eleanor, found themselves at a crossroads. Though Eleanor had dealt with much sorrow over the years—including the death of a child and Franklin's infidelity—she would later recall this as the most trying time of her life. Franklin faced this sudden tragedy with a remarkable courage and stoicism that helped to bolster Eleanor; she put her heart and soul into caring for her husband. In time, Eleanor, along with FDR's close friend and political advisor Louis Howe, came to believe that Franklin still had a bright political future ahead of him. They were determined to keep his political connections intact and do all they could to support and encourage him back into the political arena.

On June 26, 1924, Franklin returned to the limelight of national politics delivering a riveting speech nominating Al Smith at the Democratic National Convention. Though Smith lost the nomination, FDR had fought his way back into politics. It was a path that would lead him to the White House for an unprecedented four terms as president. As president, he masterfully led the country out of the Great Depression and through the darkest days of World War II. His larger-than-life personality, vigorous leadership style, and can-do spirit of optimism did much to restore hope to a forlorn nation. For her part, Eleanor became the greatest first lady the country had ever seen, a tireless humanitarian and champion for the underprivileged, and the most revered woman of her generation.

Franklin and Eleanor Roosevelt: Their Essential Wisdom gathers hundreds of memorable quotations from this fascinating and complex couple. The selections have been culled from their individual speeches, broadcasts, remarks, interviews, books, letters, and other writings. Both were prolific writers, their collective writings account for millions of pages of documents that are now housed at the Roosevelt Library in Hyde Park, New York.

The excerpts are arranged thematically and give, it is hoped, some additional insight into Franklin and Eleanor—both as a couple and as individuals—revealing their deeply held views, dynamic leadership styles, and keen political minds. In the selections, Franklin speaks passionately about America and the American way of life; he expresses his anger at the "economic royalty" whom he faults in part for America's descent into the Great Depression; and he eloquently expresses his belief that freedom will prevail with an ultimate Allied victory in World War II. Eleanor shares her fervent belief in equality for all Americans, offers insight into the realities of the peace process, and expresses her hope for an end to poverty. Elsewhere, the Roosevelts impart their singular wisdom on such subjects as the quest for freedom, the right to education, the brutalities of war, the value of history, and the meaning of true friendship.

Still other selections offer a more personal glimpse into Franklin and Eleanor's lives. During their engagement, Franklin writes to his mother of being the "happiest man just now in the world" with Eleanor; Eleanor writes Franklin ardent letters expressing her undying devotion to him. Even after years of marriage, Franklin writes lovingly to Eleanor asking about their "chicks" and expressing his longing to see her and the children. Eleanor fondly recalls family Christmas celebrations during their White House years, and thoughtfully reflects on the joys and trials of motherhood. The last chapter of the book includes quotations from family, friends, historians, writers, and politicians who share their memories and offer insights about the couple and their enduring legacies.

Franklin and Eleanor Roosevelt: Their Essential Wisdom invites readers to revisit the words of this extraordinary couple whose boundless strength, fierce determination, and bold leadership, coupled with an unabashed willingness to defy convention, left a profound mark on the history of America and the world.

—CAROL KELLY-GANGI
2014

EARLY YEARS

In thinking back to my earliest days, I am impressed by the peacefulness and regularity of things both in respect to places and people. Up to the age of seven . . . Hyde Park was the center of the world.

—Franklin D. Roosevelt

❧

Mummie, if I didn't give the orders, nothing would happen!

—Young Franklin Roosevelt's response to his mother who told him to let some of the other boys give the orders when they were building a fort

❧

My mother was one of the most beautiful women I have ever seen.

—Eleanor Roosevelt, *This Is My Story*, 1939

❧

He dominated my life as long as he lived, and was the love of my life for many years after he died.

—Eleanor Roosevelt, about her father, *This Is My Story*, 1939

It was a beautiful party, of course, but I was so unhappy, because a girl who comes out is so utterly miserable if she does not know all the young people. Of course I had been so long abroad that I had lost touch with all the girls I used to know in New York. I was miserable through all that.

—**Eleanor Roosevelt recalling her debut**

To receive a piece of jewelry from a man to whom you were not engaged was a sign of being a fast woman, and the idea that you would permit any man to kiss you before you were engaged to him never even crossed my mind.

—**Eleanor Roosevelt, *This Is My Story*, 1939**

GOVERNMENT
AND DEMOCRACY

Let us not be afraid to help each other—let us never forget that government is ourselves and not an alien power over us. The ultimate rulers of our democracy are not a President and senators and congressmen and government officials but the voters of this country.

—Franklin D. Roosevelt, speech in Marietta, Ohio, July 8, 1938

We cannot call ourselves either wise or patriotic if we seek to escape the responsibility of remolding government to make it more serviceable to all the people and more responsive to modern needs.

—Franklin D. Roosevelt, address on the finances and responsibilities of local government, University of Virginia, Charlottesville, July 6, 1931

History proves that dictatorships do not grow out of strong and successful governments, but out of weak and helpless ones. If by democratic methods people get a government strong enough to protect them from fear and starvation, their democracy succeeds; but if they do not, they grow impatient. Therefore, the only sure bulwark of continuing liberty is a government strong enough to protect the interests of the people, and a people strong enough and well enough informed to maintain its sovereign control over its government.

—Franklin D. Roosevelt, radio address, April 14, 1938

The primary concern of any Government dominated by the humane ideals of democracy is the simple principle that in a land of vast resources no one should be permitted to starve.

—Franklin D. Roosevelt, radio address,
June 28, 1934

∾

Government has a final responsibility for the well-being of its citizens. If private cooperative effort fails to provide work for willing hands and relief for the unfortunate, those suffering hardship through no fault of their own have a right to call upon the government for aid. And a government worthy of the name must make a fitting response.

—Franklin D. Roosevelt, annual message to Congress,
January 3, 1938

∾

Governments can err, Presidents do make mistakes, but the immortal Dante tells us that divine justice weighs the sins of the cold-blooded and the sins of the warm-hearted in different scales. Better the occasional faults of a Government that lives in a spirit of charity than the consistent omissions of a Government frozen in the ice of its own indifference.

—Franklin D. Roosevelt, speech accepting renomination as president,
Philadelphia, June 27, 1936

Democratic processes of government can always meet the problems of an emergency, if the leadership in public life recognizes and has the courage to tackle the problems of the day.

—Franklin D. Roosevelt, speech in Casper, Wyoming,
September 24, 1937

One of the surest safeguards of American democracy is the fact that a million young people year by year study America's historic ideals in the colleges and universities.

—Franklin D. Roosevelt, letter to the students of the University of
Pennsylvania, Philadelphia, September 26, 1935

A democratic form of government, a democratic way of life, presupposes free public education over a long period; it presupposes also an education for personal responsibility that too often is neglected.

—Eleanor Roosevelt, "Let Us Have Faith in Democracy,"
Land Policy Review, Department of Agriculture,
January 1942

Under a dictatorship it may be sufficient to learn to read and write and to do certain things by rote, but in a democracy we must learn to reason and to think for ourselves.

—Eleanor Roosevelt, quoted in *Collier's*,
June 15, 1940

The success or failure of democracy boils itself down to two things, freedom and security. Freedom boils down to a chance to work and earn a living at your work.

—Eleanor Roosevelt, White House press conference,
May 22, 1939

Democracy is not a static thing. It is an everlasting march.

—Franklin D. Roosevelt, address in Los Angeles,
October 1, 1935

AMERICA AND AMERICANS

The vigor of our history comes, largely, from the fact that, as a comparatively young nation we have gone fearlessly ahead doing things that were never done before.

—Franklin D. Roosevelt, address to the Young Democratic Club,
Baltimore, April 13, 1936

❧

Lives of Nations are determined not by the count of years, but by the lifetime of the human spirit. The life of a man is threescore years and ten: a little more, a little less. The life of a Nation is the fullness of the measure of its will to live.

—Franklin D. Roosevelt, third inaugural address,
January 20, 1941

❧

America needs a government of constant progress along liberal lines. America requires that this progress be sane and that this progress be honest. America calls for government with a soul.

—Franklin D. Roosevelt, speech in Oklahoma City,
July 9, 1938

❧

Government itself cannot close its eyes to the pollution of waters, to the erosion of soil, to the slashing of forests, any more than it can close its eyes to the need for slum clearance and schools and bridges.

—Franklin D. Roosevelt, address at dedication of the
Triborough Bridge, New York City, July 11, 1936

We believe that the material resources of America should serve the human resources of America.

—Franklin D. Roosevelt, campaign address in Providence, Rhode Island, October 21, 1936

∾

There is a mysterious cycle in human events. To some generations much is given. Of other generations much is expected. This generation of Americans has a rendezvous with destiny.

—Franklin D. Roosevelt, acceptance speech for the renomination for the presidency, Philadelphia, June 27, 1936

∾

In our personal ambitions we are individualists. But in our seeking for economic and political progress as a nation, we all go up, or else we all go down, as one people.

—Franklin D. Roosevelt, second inaugural address, January 20, 1937

∾

We are all bound together by hope of a common future rather than by reverence for a common past . . . For all our millions of square miles, for all our millions of people, there is a unity in language and speech, in law and in economics, in education and in general purpose which nowhere finds its match.

—Franklin D. Roosevelt, address on the fiftieth anniversary of the Statue of Liberty, October 28, 1936

Remember, remember always that all of us, and you and I especially, are descended from immigrants and revolutionists.

> —Franklin D. Roosevelt, address to the Daughters of the American Revolution, Washington, D.C., April 21, 1938

We are proud people, conscious of our greatness, and yet our traditions of simplicity are important to us. We want dignity but no false pomp and show.

> —Eleanor Roosevelt's newspaper column "My Day," May 18, 1949

For over three centuries a steady stream of men, women, and children followed the beacon of liberty which this light symbolizes. They brought to us a strength and moral fibre developed in a civilization centuries old, but fired anew by the dream of a better life in America. They brought to one new country the cultures of a hundred old ones.

> —Franklin D. Roosevelt, address on the fiftieth anniversary of the Statue of Liberty, October 28, 1936

I sometimes think that the saving grace of America lies in the fact that the overwhelming majority of Americans are possessed of two great qualities—a sense of humor and a sense of proportion.

> —Franklin D. Roosevelt, address on the bicentennial celebration of the founding of Georgia; Savannah, Georgia, November 18, 1933

Once I prophesied that this generation of Americans had a rendezvous with destiny. That prophecy now comes true. To us much is given; more is expected.

—Franklin D. Roosevelt, annual message to Congress, January 4, 1939

Always the heart and the soul of our country will be the heart and the soul of the common man—the men and the women who never have ceased to believe in democracy, who never have ceased to love their families, their homes, and their country.

—Franklin D. Roosevelt, campaign address in
Cleveland, November 2, 1940

The American people have a good habit—the habit of going right ahead and accomplishing the impossible.

—Franklin D. Roosevelt, address at Soldier Field,
Chicago, October 28, 1944

This country of ours is unique because we have always expected every generation of young people to do better than their parents.

—Eleanor Roosevelt, "My Day," April 17, 1944

This is . . . a trait no other nation seems to possess in quite the same degree that we do—namely, a feeling of almost childish injury and resentment unless the world as a whole recognizes how innocent we are of anything but the most generous and harmless intentions.

—Eleanor Roosevelt, "My Day," November 11, 1946

❧

We are a nation of many nationalities, many races, many religions— bound together by a single unity, the unity of freedom and equality.

Whoever seeks to set one nationality against another, seeks to degrade all nationalities.

Whoever seeks to set one race against another seeks to enslave all races.

Whoever seeks to set one religion against another, seeks to destroy all religion.

—Franklin D. Roosevelt, campaign address in Brooklyn, New York, November 1, 1940

❧

True patriotism springs from a belief in the dignity of the individual, freedom and equality not only for Americans but for all people on earth, universal brotherhood and good will, and a constant striving toward the principles and ideals on which this country was founded.

—Eleanor Roosevelt, *Eleanor Roosevelt's Book of Common Sense Etiquette*, 1962

Only with equal justice, equal opportunity, and equal participation in the government can we expect to be a united country.

—Eleanor Roosevelt, "Social Gains and Defense,"
Common Sense, March 1941

☙

Self-help and self-control are the essence of the American tradition.

—Franklin D. Roosevelt, State of the Union address, January 3, 1934

☙

The American Dream is never entirely realized.

—Eleanor Roosevelt, *The Autobiography of Eleanor Roosevelt*, 1961

☙

It seems to me that we are most completely, most loudly, most proudly American around Election Day. Because it is then that we can assert ourselves—voters and candidates alike. We can assert the most glorious, the most encouraging fact in all the world today— the fact that democracy is alive—and going strong. We are telling the world that we are free—and we intend to remain free and at peace. We are free to live and love and laugh. We face the future with confidence and courage. We are American.

—Franklin D. Roosevelt, campaign address in
Boston, October 30, 1940

POLITICS

The truth is I don't like politics especially. I probably know too much about it—and the sacrifices it demands.

—Eleanor Roosevelt, *The New York Times*, October 10, 1954

Be sincere; be brief; be seated.

—Franklin D. Roosevelt, advice to his son James on giving a speech

A radical is a man with both feet firmly planted—in the air. A conservative is a man with two perfectly good legs who, however, has never learned to walk forward. A reactionary is a somnambulist walking backwards. A liberal is a man who uses his legs and his hands at the behest—at the command—of his head.

—Franklin D. Roosevelt, radio address, October 26, 1939

I'm not the smartest fellow in the world, but I can sure pick smart colleagues.

—Franklin D. Roosevelt

I call myself a little left of center.

—Franklin D. Roosevelt, press conference, May 30, 1944

Favor comes [to the political leader] because for a brief moment in the great space of human change and progress some general human purpose finds in him a satisfactory embodiment.

—Franklin D. Roosevelt, last speech before being elected president,
Poughkeepsie, New York, November 7, 1932

∾

The whole purpose of Republican oratory these days seems to be to switch labels. The object is to persuade the American people that the Democratic Party was responsible for the 1929 crash and the depression, and that the Republican Party was responsible for all social progress under the New Deal.

—Franklin D. Roosevelt, campaign dinner address,
September 23, 1944

∾

These Republican leaders have not been content with attacks on me, or my wife, or on my sons. No, not content with that, they now include my little dog, Fala. Well, of course, I don't resent attacks, and my family doesn't resent attacks, but Fala does resent them. . . . He has not been the same dog since. I am accustomed to hearing malicious falsehoods about myself—such as that old, worm-eaten chestnut that I have represented myself as indispensable. But I think I have a right to resent, to object to libelous statements about my dog.

—Franklin D. Roosevelt, campaign dinner address,
September 23, 1944

The American people are quite competent to judge a political party that works both sides of the street.

—Franklin D. Roosevelt, campaign speech in
Boston, November 1944

❧

When people carelessly or snobbishly deride political parties, they overlook the fact that the party system of government is one of the greatest methods of unification and of teaching people to think in common terms of our civilization.

—Franklin D. Roosevelt, address at Jefferson Day dinner,
St. Paul, Minnesota, April 18, 1932

❧

It is true that we Americans have found party organizations to be useful, and indeed necessary, in the crystallization of opinion and in the demarcation of issues. It is true that I have received many honors at the hands of one of our great parties. It is nevertheless true that in the grave questions that confront the United States at this hour, I, as President of the United States, must and will consider our common problems first, foremost and preeminently from the American point of view.

—Franklin D. Roosevelt, address at Jackson Day dinner,
Washington, D.C., January 8, 1936

Consciously, I never tried to exert any political influence on my husband or on anyone else in the government. However, one cannot live in a political atmosphere and study the actions of a good politician, which my husband was, without absorbing some rudimentary facts about politics. From him I learned that a good politician is marked to a great extent by his sense of timing. He says the right thing at the right moment. . . . He could watch with enormous patience as a situation developed and wait for exactly the right moment to act or speak.

—Eleanor Roosevelt,
The Autobiography of Eleanor Roosevelt, 1961

∾

I have always felt that anyone who wanted an election so much that they would use those methods did not have the character that I really admired in public life.

—Eleanor Roosevelt commenting on Richard Nixon's
campaign against Helen Gahagan Douglas, from
Meet the Press, September 16, 1956

∾

In political life I have never felt that anything really mattered but the satisfaction of knowing that you stood for the things in which you believed, and had done the very best you could.

—Eleanor Roosevelt, "My Day,"
November 8, 1944

FREEDOM AND HUMAN RIGHTS

In the truest sense freedom cannot be bestowed; it must be achieved.

—Franklin D. Roosevelt, message on the seventy-fourth anniversary
of the Emancipation Proclamation, September 22, 1936

Liberty requires opportunity to make a living—a living decent
according to the standard of the time, a living which gives man not
only enough to live by, but something to live for.

—Franklin D. Roosevelt, acceptance speech at the Democratic
National Convention, Philadelphia, June 27, 1936

Will we ever learn to use reason instead of force in the world, and
will people ever be wise enough to refuse to follow bad leaders or
to take away the freedom of other people?

—Eleanor Roosevelt, "My Day," October 16, 1939

Franklin D. Roosevelt

In the United States we regard it as axiomatic that every person shall
enjoy the free exercise of his religion according to the dictates of his
conscience. Our flag for a century and a half has been the symbol of
the principles of liberty of conscience, of religious freedom and of
equality before the law; and these concepts are deeply ingrained in
our national character.

—Franklin D. Roosevelt, address at the
San Diego Exposition, October 2, 1935

Liberty is the air Americans breathe. Our government is based on the belief that a people can be both strong and free, that civilized men need no restraint but that imposed by themselves against abuse of freedom.

—Franklin D. Roosevelt, address at Harvard University,
Cambridge, Massachusetts, September 18, 1936

It is a good thing to demand liberty for ourselves and for those who agree with us, but it is a better thing and rarer thing to give liberty to others who do not agree with us.

—Franklin D. Roosevelt, radio address on the three hundredth
anniversary of Maryland's founding, November 22, 1933

Those who would give up essential liberty to purchase a little temporary safety deserve neither Liberty nor Safety.

—Franklin D. Roosevelt, quoting Benjamin Franklin, "The Four
Freedoms" State of the Union address, January 6, 1941

At all times, day by day, we have to continue fighting for freedom of religion, freedom of speech, and freedom from want—for these are things that must be gained in peace as well as in war.

—Eleanor Roosevelt, "My Day," April 15, 1943

In the future days, which we seek to make secure, we look forward to a world founded upon four essential human freedoms.

The first is freedom of speech and expression—everywhere in the world.

The next is freedom of every person to worship God in his own way—everywhere in the world.

The third is freedom from want—which, translated into world terms, means economic understandings which will secure to every nation a healthy peacetime life for its inhabitants—everywhere in the world.

The fourth is freedom from fear—which, translated into world terms, means a worldwide reduction of armaments to such a point and in such a thorough fashion that no nation will be in a position to commit an act of physical aggression against any neighbor—anywhere in the world.

—Franklin D. Roosevelt, "The Four Freedoms"
State of the Union address, January 6, 1941

We, too, born to freedom, and believing in freedom, are willing to fight to maintain freedom. We, and all others who believe as deeply as we do, would rather die on our feet than live on our knees.

—Franklin D. Roosevelt, address at Harvard University,
Cambridge, Massachusetts, June 19, 1941

Liberty and peace are living things. In each generation—if they are to be maintained—they must be guarded and vitalized anew.

—Franklin D. Roosevelt, address on the fiftieth anniversary
of the Statue of Liberty, October 28, 1936

Where, after all, do universal human rights begin? In small places, close to home—so close and so small that they cannot be seen on any maps of the world. Yet they are the world of the individual person; the neighborhood he lives in; the school or college he attends; the factory, farm or office where he works. Such are the places where every man, woman, and child seeks equal justice, equal opportunity, equal dignity without discrimination. Unless these rights have meaning there, they have little meaning anywhere. Without concerned citizen action to uphold them close to home, we shall look in vain for progress in the larger world.

—Eleanor Roosevelt, "The Great Question" speech at
the United Nations, New York, March 27, 1958

We cannot force people to accept friends for whom they have no liking, but living in a democracy it is entirely reasonable to demand that every citizen of that democracy enjoy the fundamental rights of a citizen.

—Eleanor Roosevelt, "Race, Religion, and Prejudice,"
New Republic, May 11, 1942

Freedom means the supremacy of human rights everywhere. Our support goes to those who struggle to gain those rights or keep them.

—Franklin D. Roosevelt, "The Four Freedoms"
State of the Union address, January 6, 1941

EQUALITY, THE LAW,
AND JUSTICE

We know that equality of individual ability has never existed and never will, but we do insist that equality of opportunity still must be sought. We know that equality of local justice is, alas, not yet an established fact; this also is a goal we must and do seek.

—Franklin D. Roosevelt, address on the centennial of Arkansas' admission into the Union, Little Rock, Arkansas, June 10, 1936

Inside the polling booth every American man and woman stands as the equal of every other American man and woman. There they have no superiors. There they have no masters save their own minds and consciences. There they are sovereign American citizens.

—Franklin D. Roosevelt, campaign address in Worcester, Massachusetts, October 21, 1936

No democracy can long survive which does not accept as fundamental to its very existence the recognition of the rights of minorities.

—Franklin D. Roosevelt, letter to the NAACP, June 25, 1938

We must be proud of every one of our citizens, for regardless of nationality, or race, every one contributes to the welfare and culture of the nation.

—Eleanor Roosevelt, speech at the Southern Conference on Human Welfare, November 1938

I believe that it is essential to our leadership in the world and to the development of true democracy in our country to have no discrimination in our country whatsoever. This is most important in the schools of our country.

—Eleanor Roosevelt, letter to Richard Bolling,
January 20, 1956

It is our duty to make sure that, big as this country is, there is no room for racial or religious intolerance—and that there is no room for snobbery.

—Franklin D. Roosevelt, address at Fenway Park,
Boston, November 4, 1944

We never know where prejudices will lead us. Neither do we know how often we use our prejudices to excuse or cloak motives and emotions which we would be ashamed to bring into the light of day.

—Eleanor Roosevelt, "My Day," December 16, 1944

Among American citizens, there should be no forgotten men and no forgotten races.

—Franklin D. Roosevelt,
October 26, 1936

Too often the great decisions are originated and given form in bodies made up wholly of men, or so completely dominated by them that whatever of special value women have to offer is shunted aside without expression.

> —Eleanor Roosevelt, speech, United Nations,
> December 1952

❧

In numbers there is strength, and we in America must help the women of the world.

> —Eleanor Roosevelt, "My Day," October 22, 1946

❧

A woman will always have to be better than a man in any job she undertakes.

> —Eleanor Roosevelt, "My Day," November 29, 1945

❧

If women do the same work I have always believed that they should receive the same pay.

> —Eleanor Roosevelt, "If You Ask Me," *Ladies Home Journal*,
> March 1944

The United States Constitution has proved itself the most marvelously elastic compilation of rules of government ever written.

—Franklin D. Roosevelt, radio broadcast, March 2, 1930

Our Constitution is so simple and practical that it is possible always to meet extraordinary needs by changes in emphasis and arrangement without loss of essential form. That is why our constitutional system has proved itself the most superbly enduring political mechanism the modern world has produced.

—Franklin D. Roosevelt, first inaugural address, March 4, 1933

On this solemn anniversary I ask that the American people rejoice in the wisdom of their Constitution. I ask that they guarantee the effectiveness of each of its parts by living by the Constitution as a whole. . . . I ask that they give their fealty to the Constitution itself and not to its misinterpreters. I ask that they exalt the glorious simplicity of its purposes, rather than a century of complicated legalism. I ask that majorities and minorities subordinate intolerance and power alike to the common good of all. For us the Constitution is a common bond, without bitterness, for those who see America as Lincoln saw it, "the last, best hope of earth." So we revere it, not because it is old but because it is ever new, not in the worship of its past alone but in the faith of the living who keep it young, now and in the years to come.

—Franklin D. Roosevelt, address on Constitution Day,
Washington, D.C., September 17, 1937

The Constitution of the United States was a layman's document, not a lawyer's contract. That cannot be stressed too often.

—Franklin D. Roosevelt, address on Constitution Day,
Washington, D.C., September 17, 1937

∽

Justice cannot be for one side alone, but must be for both.

—Eleanor Roosevelt, "My Day," October 14, 1947

∽

Like all lawyers, like all Americans, I regret the necessity of this controversy. But the welfare of the United States, and indeed of the Constitution itself, is what we all must think about first. Our difficulty with the Court today rises not from the Court as an institution but from human beings within it. But we cannot yield our constitutional destiny to the personal judgment of a few men who, being fearful of the future, would deny us the necessary means of dealing with the present.

—Franklin D. Roosevelt, radio address discussing his
plan to "pack" the Supreme Court, March 9, 1937

∽

The attitude of the Supreme Court toward constitutional questions is entirely changed. Its recent decisions are eloquent testimony of a willingness to collaborate with the two other branches of government to make democracy work.

—Franklin D. Roosevelt, radio address, June 24, 1938

We must scrupulously guard the civil rights and civil liberties of all citizens, whatever their background. We must remember that any oppression, any injustice, any hatred, is a wedge designed to attack our civilization.

—Franklin D. Roosevelt, greeting to the American Committee for Protection of Foreign-born, January 9, 1940

In these days of difficulty, we Americans everywhere must and shall choose the path of social justice . . . the path of faith, the path of hope, and the path of love toward our fellow man.

—Franklin D. Roosevelt, campaign address, Detroit, Michigan, October 2, 1932

You have set an example which seems to me unfortunate, and I feel obliged to send in to you my resignation.

—Eleanor Roosevelt, letter to the Daughters of the American Revolution, which refused to allow Marian Anderson to sing at Constitution Hall because of her race, February 26, 1939

PRESIDENT AND
FIRST LADY

What a weight of responsibility this one man at the desk, facing the rest of the people, has to carry. Not just for this hemisphere alone, but for the world as a whole!

—Eleanor Roosevelt, "My Day," May 29, 1941

෴

I never forget that I live in a house owned by all the American people and that I have been given their trust.

—Franklin D. Roosevelt, radio address,
April 14, 1938

෴

The Presidency is not merely an administrative office. That's the least of it. It is more than an engineering job, efficient or inefficient. It is preeminently a place of moral leadership. All our great Presidents were leaders of thought at times when certain historic ideas in the life of the nation had to be clarified. . . . Isn't that what the office is—a superb opportunity for reapplying, applying in new conditions, the simple rules of human conduct we always go back to?

—Franklin D. Roosevelt, *The New York Times Magazine*,
September 11, 1932

෴

Power must be linked with responsibility and obliged to defend and justify itself within the framework of the general good.

—Franklin D. Roosevelt, State of the Union address,
January 6, 1945

No man can occupy the office of President without realizing that he is President of all the people.

—Franklin D. Roosevelt, address at Madison Square Garden,
New York City, October 31, 1936

❧

The Presidency carries with it, for the time being, the leadership of a political party as well. But the Presidency carries with it a far higher obligation than this—the duty of analyzing and setting forth national needs and ideals which transcend and cut across all lines of party affiliation.

—Franklin D. Roosevelt, address to the Young Democratic
Clubs of America, August 24, 1935

❧

One thing is sure. We have to do something. We have to do the best we know how at the moment. . . . If it doesn't turn out right, we can modify it as we go along.

—Franklin D. Roosevelt, advice to Secretary of Labor
Frances Perkins, 1933

❧

The loneliest feeling in the world is when you think you are leading the parade and turn to find that no one is following you. No president who badly misguesses public opinion will last very long.

—Franklin D. Roosevelt, recalled by his Secretary of Labor
Frances Perkins, interview, University of Illinois, 1958

Wise and prudent men—intelligent conservatives—have long known that in a changing world worthy institutions can be conserved only by adjusting them to the changing times. In the words of the great essayist, "The voice of great events is proclaiming to us. Reform if you would preserve." I am that kind of conservative because I am that kind of liberal.

—Franklin D. Roosevelt, address before the Democratic state convention,
Syracuse, New York, September 29, 1936

I have no expectation of making a hit every time I come to bat. What I seek is the highest possible batting average, not only for myself, but for my team.

—Franklin D. Roosevelt, radio address, 1933

We may make mistakes—but they must never be mistakes which result from faintness of heart or abandonment of moral principle.

—Franklin D. Roosevelt, fourth inaugural address, January 20, 1945

All that is within me cries out to go back to my home on the Hudson River, to avoid public responsibilities, and to avoid also the publicity which in our democracy follows every step of the Nation's Chief Executive.

—Franklin D. Roosevelt, letter agreeing to accept nomination
for fourth term as president, July 11, 1944

I know Franklin always gave thought to what people said, but I have never known anyone less influenced by others. Though he asked for advice from a great many people, he simply wanted points of view which might help him to form his final decision, and which he sifted through his own knowledge and feelings. But once he reached a decision, people flattered themselves if they thought they ever changed it.

—Eleanor Roosevelt, *The Autobiography of Eleanor Roosevelt*, 1961

I'm just afraid that I may not have the strength to do this job. After you leave me tonight, Jimmy, I am going to pray. I am going to pray that God will help me, that he will give me the strength and the guidance to do this job and to do it right. I hope that you will pray for me, too, Jimmy.

—Franklin D. Roosevelt, to his son James
on election night, November 8, 1932

It is the duty of the President to propose and it is the privilege of the Congress to dispose.

—Franklin D. Roosevelt, press conference, December 29, 1933

Almost any woman in the White House during these years of need would have done what I have done—tried to help.

—Eleanor Roosevelt, *The New York Times*, January 25, 1941

I have all the pomp & restriction & none of the power!

—Eleanor Roosevelt, letter to Joseph P. Lash,
September 6, 1943

∿

I never urged on him a specific course of action, no matter how strongly I felt, because I realized he knew of factors in the picture as a whole of which I might be ignorant.

—Eleanor Roosevelt, *This I Remember*, 1949

∿

Criticism . . . makes very little dent upon me, unless I think there is some real justification and something should be done.

—Eleanor Roosevelt, in a letter to feminist
Carrie Chapman Catt, April 18, 1936

∿

You will find that [as the First Lady] you are no longer clothing yourself, you are dressing a public monument.

—Eleanor Roosevelt, *New York Herald Tribune*,
October 27, 1960

I am still taken aback to discover how closely one's most trivial moments are followed in this day of television. It seems as though one can find privacy only within the silence of one's own mind.

—Eleanor Roosevelt, *The Autobiography of Eleanor Roosevelt*, 1961

Today, in this year of war, 1945, we have learned lessons—at a fearful cost—and we shall profit by them. We have learned that we cannot live alone, at peace; that our own well-being is dependent on the well-being of other Nations, far away. We have learned that we must live as men and not as ostriches, nor as dogs in the manger. We have learned to be citizens of the world, members of the human community. We have learned the simple truth, as Emerson said, that, "The only way to have a friend is to be one."

—Franklin D. Roosevelt, fourth inaugural address,
January 20, 1945

THE GREAT DEPRESSION
AND THE NEW DEAL

The country needs and, unless I mistake its temper, the country demands bold persistent experimentation. It is common sense to take a method and try it. If it fails, admit it frankly and try another. But above all, try something.

—Franklin D. Roosevelt, commencement address,
Oglethorpe University, Atlanta, May 22, 1932

These unhappy times call for the building of plans that rest upon the forgotten, the unorganized but the indispensable units of economic power, for plans like those of 1917 that build from the bottom up and not from the top down, that put their faith once more in the forgotten man at the bottom of the economic pyramid.

—Franklin D. Roosevelt, "The Forgotten Man Speech"
radio address, April 7, 1932

What do the people of America want more than anything else? In my mind, two things: Work; work, with all the moral and spiritual values that go with work. And with work, a reasonable measure of security—security for themselves and for their wives and children. Work and security—these are more than words. They are more than facts. They are the spiritual values, the true goal toward which our efforts of reconstruction should lead.

—Franklin D. Roosevelt, speech to Democratic National
Convention accepting the presidential
nomination, Chicago, July 2, 1932

We need enthusiasm, imagination and the ability to face facts, even unpleasant ones, bravely. We need to correct, by drastic means if necessary, the faults in our economic system from which we now suffer. We need the courage of the young.

—Franklin D. Roosevelt, commencement address,
Oglethorpe University, Atlanta, May 22, 1932

❧

I pledge you, I pledge myself, to a new deal for the American people.

—Franklin D. Roosevelt, speech to Democratic National Convention
accepting the presidential nomination, Chicago, July 2, 1932

❧

Faith is a delicate though powerful factor in our economic life, and a party that sounds a note of alarm from high places is performing no decent service to the American nation.

—Franklin D. Roosevelt, campaign address,
St. Louis, October 21, 1932

❧

This great nation will endure as it has endured, will revive and will prosper. So, first of all, let me assert my firm belief that the only thing we have to fear is fear itself—nameless, unreasoning, unjustified terror which paralyzes needed efforts to convert retreat into advance.

—Franklin D. Roosevelt, first inaugural address,
March 4, 1933

Our greatest primary task is to put people to work. This is no unsolvable problem if we face it wisely and courageously. It can be accomplished in part by direct recruiting by the Government itself, treating the task as we would treat the emergency of a war, but at the same time, through this employment, accomplishing greatly needed projects to stimulate and reorganize the use of our natural resources.

—Franklin D. Roosevelt, first inaugural address,
March 4, 1933

∾

It is the right of old people when they have worked hard all their lives, and, through no fault of theirs, have not been able to provide for their old age, to be cared for in the last years of their life.

—Eleanor Roosevelt, speech to chapter of the
American Association for Social Security,
Washington, D.C., February 8, 1934

∾

We can never insure one hundred percent of the population against one hundred percent of the hazards and vicissitudes of life, but we have tried to frame a law which will give some measure of protection to the average citizen and to his family against the loss of a job and against poverty-ridden old age.

—Franklin D. Roosevelt, presidential statement signing
the Social Security Act, August 14, 1935

No country, however rich, can afford the waste of its human resources. Demoralization caused by vast unemployment is our greatest extravagance. Morally, it is the greatest menace to our social order.

—Franklin D. Roosevelt, radio address,
September 30, 1934

The simplest way for each of you to judge recovery lies in the plain facts of your own individual situation. Are you better off than you were last year? Are your debts less burdensome? Is your bank account more secure? Are your working conditions better? Is your faith in your own individual future more firmly grounded?

—Franklin D. Roosevelt, radio address, June 28, 1934

The right to work seems to me as vital a part of our freedom as any right which we may have.

—Eleanor Roosevelt, *Woman's Home Companion*,
November 1933

Men and nature must work hand in hand. The throwing out of balance of the resources of nature throws out of balance also the lives of men.

—Franklin D. Roosevelt, message to Congress on the use
of our national resources, January 24, 1935

I see one-third of a nation ill-housed, ill-clad, ill-nourished. . . .
The test of our progress is not whether we add more to the
abundance of those who have much; it is whether we provide
enough for those who have too little.

—Franklin D. Roosevelt, second inaugural address,
January 20, 1937

∾

Millions today are living in urban and rural habitations which fail
to comply with minimum standards of health, safety and decency.
The continued existence of these conditions breeds disease and
crime and impairs the health and vitality of our present and future
generations.

—Franklin D. Roosevelt, letter to governors of several
states urging housing legislation, March 1, 1938

∾

The greatest single resource of this country is its youth, and no
progressive government can afford to ignore the needs of its future
citizens for adequate schooling and for that useful work which
establishes them as part of its economy. To ignore this need is to
undermine the very basis of democracy which requires the constant
renewal of its vitality through the absorption of its young people.

—Franklin D. Roosevelt, message to Congress requesting
appropriations for work relief, April 27, 1939

Words come easily, but they do not change the record. You are, most of you, old enough to remember what things were like for labor in 1932. You remember the closed banks and the breadlines and the starvation wages; the foreclosures of homes and farms, and the bankruptcies of business; the "Hoovervilles," and the young men and women of the Nation facing a hopeless, jobless future; the closed factories and mines and mills; the ruined and abandoned farms; the stalled railroads and the empty docks; the blank despair of a whole Nation—and the utter impotence of the Federal Government.

—Franklin D. Roosevelt, campaign dinner address,
September 23, 1944

We have our difficulties, true—but we are a wiser and a tougher nation than we were in 1929, or in 1932.

—Franklin D. Roosevelt, annual message to Congress, 1939

THE ECONOMY, BUSINESS, AND LABOR

Depression will be avoided if our financial and economic powers in our countries can understand that greed cannot be the motivating force.

—Eleanor Roosevelt, *The New York Times*, January 9, 1948

∾

The first theory is that if we make the rich richer, somehow they will let a part of their prosperity trickle down to the rest of us. The second theory was the theory that if we make the average of mankind comfortable and secure, their prosperity will rise upward through the ranks.

—Franklin D. Roosevelt, campaign address,
Detroit, October 2, 1932

∾

But while they prate of economic laws, men and women are starving. We must lay hold of the fact that economic laws are not made by nature. They are made by human beings.

—Franklin D. Roosevelt speech to Democratic National
Convention accepting the presidential nomination,
Chicago, July 2, 1932

∾

Concentration of economic power in all-embracing corporations . . . represents private enterprise which has become a kind of private government which is a power unto itself—a regimentation of other people's money and other people's lives.

—Franklin D. Roosevelt, speech accepting renomination
as president, Philadelphia, June 27, 1936

You cannot borrow your way out of debt: but you can invest your way into a sounder future.

—Franklin D. Roosevelt, address,
Atlanta, November 29, 1935

❧

Private enterprise, indeed, became too private. It became privileged enterprise, not free enterprise.

—Franklin D. Roosevelt, speech accepting renomination
as president, Philadelphia, June 27, 1936

❧

We have always known that heedless self-interest was bad morals; we now know that it is bad economics. Out of the collapse of a prosperity whose builders boasted their practicality has come the conviction that in the long run economic morality pays.

—Franklin D. Roosevelt, second inaugural address,
January 20, 1937

❧

The hours men and women worked, the wages they received, the conditions of their labor—these had passed beyond the control of the people, and were imposed by this new industrial dictatorship. The savings of the average family, the capital of the small-businessmen, the investments set aside for old age—other people's money—these were tools which the new economic royalty used to dig itself in.

—Franklin D. Roosevelt, speech accepting renomination
as president, Philadelphia, June 27, 1936

I want to preach a new doctrine. A complete separation of business and government.

> —Franklin D. Roosevelt, dedication speech at Tammany Hall's
> new headquarters, New York City, July 4, 1929

In my Inaugural I laid down the simple proposition that nobody is going to starve in this country. It seems to me to be equally plain that no business which depends for existence on paying less than living wages to its workers has any right to continue in this country. By "business" I mean the whole of commerce as well as the whole of industry; by workers I mean all workers, the white collar class as well as the men in overalls; and by living wages I mean more than a bare subsistence level—I mean the wages of decent living.

> —Franklin D. Roosevelt, statement on the National
> Industrial Recovery Act, June 16, 1933

This concentration of wealth and power has been built upon other people's money, other people's business, other people's labor. Under this concentration independent business was allowed to exist only by sufferance. It has been a menace to the social system as well as to the economic system which we call American democracy.

> —Franklin D. Roosevelt, campaign speech,
> Chicago, October 14, 1936

I believe, I have always believed, and I will always believe in private enterprise as the backbone of economic well-being in the United States.

—Franklin D. Roosevelt, campaign address,
Chicago, October 14, 1936

A better relationship between labor and management is the high purpose of this Act. By assuring the employees the right of collective bargaining it fosters the development of the employment contract on a sound and equitable basis. By providing an orderly procedure for determining who is entitled to represent the employees, it aims to remove one of the chief causes of wasteful economic strife. By preventing practices which tend to destroy the independence of labor, it seeks, for every worker within its scope, that freedom of choice and action which is justly his.

—Franklin D. Roosevelt, upon signing the National Labor Relations Act
(Wagner Act) into law, July 5, 1935

And small business will continue to be protected from selfish and cold-blooded monopolies and cartels. Beware of that profound enemy of the free enterprise system who pays lip-service to free competition—but also labels every antitrust prosecution as a "persecution."

—Franklin D. Roosevelt, campaign address on
"Economic Bill of Rights," October 28, 1944

Cooperation with labor as well as with business is essential to the continuation of the programs we are working out for a more stable and more satisfactory industrial life in this country. I have on a number of occasions urged the necessity, as well as the soundness, of furthering the principle of collective bargaining as between labor and management.

—Franklin D. Roosevelt, greeting to the American
Federation of Labor, February 11, 1935

∾

It is now beyond partisan controversy that it is a fundamental individual right of a worker to associate himself with other workers and to bargain collectively with his employer.

—Franklin D. Roosevelt, address at San Diego Exposition,
October 2, 1935

∾

Enlightened business is learning that competition ought not to cause bad social consequences which inevitably react upon the profits of business itself. All but the hopelessly reactionary will agree that to conserve our primary resources of man power, government must have some control over maximum hour, minimum wages, the evil of child labor and the exploitation of unorganized labor.

—Franklin D. Roosevelt, "A Fair Day's Pay for a
Fair Day's Work" speech, May 24, 1937

If I went to work in a factory the first thing I'd do is join a union.

—Franklin D. Roosevelt, widely attributed

❧

Goods produced under conditions which do not meet a rudimentary standard to decency should be regarded as contraband and not allowed to pollute the channels of international commerce.

—Franklin D. Roosevelt, message to Congress,
May 24, 1937

❧

It is one of the characteristics of a free and democratic modern nation that it have free and independent labor unions.

—Franklin D. Roosevelt, speech before Teamsters
Union Convention, Washington, D.C.,
September 11, 1940

WORLD WAR II

The man is a menace.

> —Franklin D. Roosevelt's remarks to Eleanor after hearing
> Adolf Hitler's first speech as chancellor of Germany in 1933

I have made it clear that the United States cannot take part in
political arrangements in Europe, but that we stand ready to
cooperate at any time in practicable measures on a world basis
looking to immediate reduction of armaments and the lowering
of the barriers against commerce.

> —Franklin D. Roosevelt, State of the Union address, January 3, 1934

Resolute in our determination to respect the rights of others, and
to command respect for the rights of ourselves, we must keep
ourselves adequately strong in self-defense.

> —Franklin D. Roosevelt, State of the Union address, January 3, 1938

We must be the great arsenal of democracy. For us this is an
emergency as serious as war itself. We must apply ourselves to our
task with the same resolution, the same sense of urgency, the same
spirit of patriotism and sacrifice as we would show were we at war.

> —Franklin D. Roosevelt, radio address, December 29, 1940

While we, as a nation, are neutral in the present tragic war in Europe, I am sure we cannot be indifferent to the suffering inflicted upon the peoples of the war-torn countries, particularly upon the helpless women and children. It is traditional that the American people should wish, after providing in full measure for the support of our necessary charitable endeavors at home, to extend material aid to the helpless victims of war abroad.

—Franklin D. Roosevelt, appeal for coordination
of war relief agencies, October 12, 1939

The Soviet Union, as everybody who has the courage to face the fact knows, is run by a dictatorship as absolute as any other dictatorship in the world.

—Franklin D. Roosevelt, address to the American
Youth Congress, February 10, 1940

These are bad days for all of us who remember always that when real world forces come into conflict, the final result is never as dark as we mortals guess it in very difficult days.

—Franklin D. Roosevelt, letter to Joseph P. Kennedy, United
States ambassador to Great Britain, May 3, 1940

I have said this before, but I shall say it again and again and again:
Your boys are not going to be sent into any foreign wars.

—Franklin D. Roosevelt, speech,
Boston, October 30, 1940

No man can tame a tiger into a kitten by stroking it. There can be
no appeasement with ruthlessness. There can be no reasoning with an
incendiary bomb. We know now that a nation can have peace with
the Nazis only at the price of total surrender.

—Franklin D. Roosevelt, radio address, December 29, 1940

Let us say to the democracies: "We Americans are vitally concerned
in your defense of freedom. We are putting forth our energies,
our resources and our organizing powers to give you the strength
to regain and maintain a free world. We shall send you, in ever-
increasing numbers, ships, planes, tanks, guns. This is our purpose
and our pledge."

—Franklin D. Roosevelt, "The Four Freedoms"
State of the Union address, January 6, 1941

When you see a rattlesnake poised to strike, you do not wait until
he has struck before you crush him.

—Franklin D. Roosevelt, radio address, September 11, 1941

As a nation we may take pride in the fact that we are soft-hearted; but we can not afford to be soft-headed. We must always be wary of those who with sounding brass and a tinkling cymbal preach the ism of appeasement. We must especially beware of that small group of selfish men who would clip the wings of the American eaglet to feather their own nests.

—Franklin D. Roosevelt, "The Four Freedoms"
State of the Union address, January 6, 1941

And I am sure that even now the Nazis are waiting to see whether the United States will by silence give them the green light to go ahead on this path of destruction. The Nazi danger to our Western World has long ceased to be a mere possibility. The danger is here now—not only from a military enemy but from an enemy of all law, all liberty, all morality, all religion. . . . Normal practices of diplomacy—note writing—are of no possible use in dealing with international outlaws who sink our ships and kill our citizens. One peaceful nation after another has met disaster because each refused to look the Nazi danger squarely in the eye until it actually had them by the throat. The United States will not make that fatal mistake.

—Franklin D. Roosevelt, radio address on the sinking of
the *U.S.S. Greer* by the Nazis, September 11, 1941

When the dictators, if the dictators, are ready to make war upon us, they will not wait for an act of war on our part.

—Franklin D. Roosevelt, "The Four Freedoms"
State of the Union address, January 6, 1941

Against naked force the only possible defense is naked force. The aggressor makes the rules for such a war; the defenders have no alternative but matching destruction with more destruction, slaughter with greater slaughter.

—Franklin D. Roosevelt, message to the National Convention
of Young Democrats, Louisville, Kentucky, August 21, 1941

❧

Yesterday, December 7, 1941—a date which will live in infamy— the United States of America was suddenly and deliberately attacked by naval and air forces of the Empire of Japan.

—Franklin D. Roosevelt, address to joint session
of Congress asking for declaration of war
on Japan, December 8, 1941

❧

No matter how long it may take us to overcome this premeditated invasion, the American people in their righteous might will win through to absolute victory. I believe that I interpret the will of the Congress and of the people when I assert that we will not only defend ourselves to the uttermost but will make it very certain that this form of treachery shall never again endanger us.

—Franklin D. Roosevelt, address to joint session
of Congress asking for declaration of war
on Japan, December 8, 1941

I can handle that old buzzard.

—Franklin D. Roosevelt, referring to Joseph Stalin prior to their first
meeting at the Tehran Conference on November 28, 1943

There never has been—there never can be—successful compromise
between good and evil. Only total victory can reward the champions
of tolerance and decency and freedom and faith.

—Franklin D. Roosevelt, State of the Union address, January 6, 1942

We are beginning to realize, I think, as the days go on, that this
war is on a vaster scale than anything which we have ever dreamed
of before.

—Eleanor Roosevelt, "My Day," January 3, 1942

I just have a hunch that Stalin is not that kind of man. Harry
[Hopkins] says he's not and that he doesn't want anything except
security for his own country, and I think that if I give him everything
I possibly can and ask nothing from him in return, noblesse oblige,
he won't try to annex anything and will work with me for a world of
democracy and peace.

—Franklin D. Roosevelt, responding to Ambassador William C. Bullitt's
advice about a containment policy against the Soviet Union, 1943,
quoted in *Life*, August 23, 1948

We have faith that future generations will know here, in the middle
of the twentieth century, there came a time when men of good will found
a way to unite, and produce, and fight to destroy the forces
of ignorance, and intolerance, and slavery, and war.

—Franklin D. Roosevelt, address to the White House Correspondents'
Association, Washington, D.C., February 12, 1943

Almighty God: Our sons, pride of our Nation, this day have set upon
a mighty endeavor, a struggle to preserve our Republic, our religion,
and our civilization, and to set free a suffering humanity. Lead them
straight and true; give strength to their arms, stoutness to their hearts,
steadfastness in their faith. They will need Thy blessings. Their road
will be long and hard. For the enemy is strong. He may hurl back
our forces. Success may not come with rushing speed, but we shall
return again and again; and we know that by Thy grace, and by the
righteousness of our cause, our sons will triumph. They will be sore
tried, by night and by day, without rest—until the victory is won.
The darkness will be rent by noise and flame. Men's souls will be
shaken with the violences of war. For these men are lately drawn from
the ways of peace. They fight not for the lust of conquest. They fight
to end conquest. They fight to liberate. They fight to let justice arise,
and tolerance and good will among all Thy people. They yearn but for
the end of battle, for their return to the haven of home. Some will never
return. Embrace these, Father, and receive them, Thy heroic servants,
into Thy kingdom. And for us at home—fathers, mothers, children,
wives, sisters, and brothers of brave men overseas—whose thoughts
and prayers are ever with them—help us, Almighty God, to rededicate
ourselves in renewed faith in Thee in this hour of great sacrifice. . . .

—Franklin D. Roosevelt, prayer on D-Day, June 6, 1944

What has been done in the United States since those days of 1940—when France fell—in raising and equipping and transporting our fighting forces, and in producing weapons and supplies for war, has been nothing short of a miracle. It was largely due to American teamwork—teamwork among capital and labor and agriculture, between the armed forces and the civilian economy—indeed among all of them. And every one—every man or woman or child who bought a war bond helped—and helped mightily!

—Franklin D. Roosevelt, radio address, June 12, 1944

That task that we Americans now face will test us to the uttermost. Never before have we been called upon for such a prodigious effort. Never before have we had so little time in which to do so much. "These are the times that try men's souls."

—Franklin D. Roosevelt, radio address, February 23, 1942

To the Hitlerites, their subordinates and functionaries and satellites, to the German people and to all other peoples under the Nazi yoke, we have made clear our determination to punish all participants in these acts of savagery.

—Franklin D. Roosevelt, message to Congress
on refugee policy, June 12, 1944

We have astonished the world and confounded our enemies with our stupendous war production, with the overwhelming courage and skill of our fighting men—with the bridge of ships carrying our munitions and men through the seven seas—with our gigantic Fleet which has pounded the enemy all over the Pacific and has just driven through for a touchdown.

—Franklin D. Roosevelt, campaign address on the
"Economic Bill of Rights," October 28, 1944

There is going to be stern punishment for all those in Germany directly responsible for this agony of mankind. The German people are not going to be enslaved—because the United Nations do not traffic in human slavery. But it will be necessary for them to earn their way back into the fellowship of peace-loving and law-abiding nations. And, in their climb up that steep road, we shall certainly see to it that they are not encumbered by having to carry guns. They will be relieved of that burden—we hope, forever.

—Franklin D. Roosevelt, address before the Foreign Policy
Association, New York City, October 21, 1944

It would be pleasant to close our eyes and ears now and say: "These things could never be. Human beings could not do such things, and therefore we will not believe them or listen to them." That would be an easy way out because we would not have to decide how we could prevent any recurrence in the future, in any part of the world.

—Eleanor Roosevelt, "My Day," May 2, 1945

The once powerful, malignant Nazi state is crumbling. The Japanese war lords are receiving, in their own homeland, the retribution for which they asked when they attacked Pearl Harbor. But the mere conquest of our enemies is not enough. We must go on to do all in our power to conquer the doubts and the fears, the ignorance and the greed, which made this horror possible.

—Franklin D. Roosevelt, undelivered address
prepared for Jefferson Day, April 13, 1945

❧

There must be joy, of course, in the hearts of the peoples whom the Nazis conquered and who are now free again. Freedom without bread, however, has little meaning.

—Eleanor Roosevelt, reflecting on V.E. Day,
"My Day," May 9, 1945

❧

The war is over. We will not be engaged in the business of killing each other. Mass murder is ended, and we can rejoice.

—Eleanor Roosevelt, "My Day,"
August 18, 1945

EDUCATION, KNOWLEDGE, AND INFORMATION

Democracy cannot succeed unless those who express their choice are prepared to choose wisely. The real safeguard of democracy, therefore, is education.

—Franklin D. Roosevelt, message for American Education Week,
September 27, 1938

❧

In a democracy such as ours, the education of all the people is a vital necessity. They cannot become articulate and express their beliefs unless they can both write and speak.

—Eleanor Roosevelt, "My Day," November 3, 1945

❧

The school is the last expenditure upon which America should be willing to economize.

—Franklin D. Roosevelt, campaign address in
Kansas City, October 13, 1936

❧

No group and no government can properly prescribe precisely what should constitute the body of knowledge with which true education is concerned.

—Franklin D. Roosevelt, speech to National Education Association,
June 30, 1938

Men are not prisoners of fate, but only prisoners of their own minds.

—Franklin D. Roosevelt, Pan American Day address,
April 15, 1939

❧

Knowledge—that is, education in its true sense—is our best protection against unreasoning prejudice and panic-making fear, whether engendered by special interests, illiberal minorities, or panic-stricken leaders.

—Franklin D. Roosevelt, campaign address in
Boston, October 31, 1932

❧

We all know that books burn—yet we have the greater knowledge that books can not be killed by fire. People die, but books never die. No man and no force can abolish memory. No man and no force can put thought in a concentration camp forever. No man and no force can take from the world the books that embody man's eternal fight against tyranny of every kind. In this war, we know, books are weapons. And it is a part of your dedication always to make them weapons for man's freedom.

—Franklin D. Roosevelt, message to the Booksellers of America, 1942

The great achievements of science and even of art can be used in one way or another to destroy as well as create; they are only instruments by which men try to do the things they most want to do. If death is desired, science can do that. If a full, rich, and useful life is sought, science can do that also.

> —Franklin D. Roosevelt, address before the Eighth Pan American
> Scientific Conference, Washington, D.C., May 10, 1940

The constant free flow of communication among us—enabling the free interchange of ideas—forms the very blood stream of our nation. It keeps the mind and the body of our democracy eternally vital, eternally young.

> —Franklin D. Roosevelt, radio address to
> the *New York Herald Tribune* Forum,
> October 24, 1940

We must join in an effort to use all knowledge for the good of all human beings. When we do that we shall have nothing to fear.

> —Eleanor Roosevelt, *On My Own*, 1958

WEALTH AND POVERTY

Happiness lies not in the mere possession of money; it lies in the joy of achievement, in the thrill of creative effort. The joy and moral stimulation of work no longer must be forgotten in the mad chase of evanescent profits.

—Franklin D. Roosevelt, first inaugural address, March 4, 1933

I need not tell you that true wealth is not a static thing. It is a living thing made out of the disposition of men to create and to distribute the good things of life with rising standards of living. Wealth grows when men cooperate; but it stagnates in an atmosphere of misunderstanding and misrepresentation. Here, in America, the material means are at hand for the growth of true wealth. It is in the spirit of American institutions that wealth should come as the reward of hard labor—hard labor, I repeat—of mind and hand. That is a pretty good definition of what we call the profit system.

—Franklin D. Roosevelt, address before the District of
Columbia Bankers' convention, Washington, D.C.,
October 24, 1934

Poverty anywhere constitutes a danger to prosperity everywhere.

—Franklin D. Roosevelt, address to Conference of International Labor
Organization, Washington, D.C., May 17, 1944

The Delanos were the first people I met who were able to do what they wanted to do without wondering where to obtain the money, and it was not long before I learned the reason for this. My mother-in-law taught me, but I am sure that any member of her family could have taught me just as well. They watched their pennies, which I had always seen squandered. They were generous and could afford to be in big things, because so little was ever wasted or spent in inconsequential ways.

—Eleanor Roosevelt, *The Autobiography of Eleanor Roosevelt*, 1961

༃

We may pay high taxes, but if it means that many hard working people have better lives, then I am glad to do so.

—Eleanor Roosevelt, "My Day," May 31, 1937

༃

Here is my principle: Taxes shall be levied according to ability to pay. That is the only American principle.

—Franklin D. Roosevelt, address at Worcester, Massachusetts, October 21, 1936

༃

Those who have long enjoyed such privileges as we enjoy, forget in time that men have died to win them.

—Franklin D. Roosevelt, November 27, 1941

Could we have the vision of doing away in this great country with poverty? It would be a marvelous achievement. . . . That would be one of the very best arguments against Communism that we could possibly have.

—Eleanor Roosevelt, speech, Democratic
National Convention, August 13, 1956

It is an unfortunate human failing that a full pocketbook often groans more loudly than an empty stomach. I am, as you know, a firm believer in private enterprise and in private property. I am a firm believer in the American opportunity of men and women to rise in private enterprise. But, of course, if private opportunity is to remain safe, average men and women must be able to have it as a part of their own individual satisfaction in life and their own stake in democracy.

—Franklin D. Roosevelt, campaign address,
Brooklyn, New York, November 1, 1940

We cannot exist as a little island of well-being in a world where two-thirds of the people go to bed hungry every night.

—Eleanor Roosevelt, speech, Democratic fundraising dinner,
December 8, 1959

Real prosperity can only come out when everybody prospers.

—Eleanor Roosevelt, "My Day," March 19, 1936

PEACE, WAR, AND FOREIGN POLICY

Peace depends upon the acceptance of the principle and practice of the good neighbor. The practice is founded on the golden rule, and must be fortified by cooperation of every kind between nations.

—Franklin D. Roosevelt, campaign address in
St. Paul, October 9, 1936

❧

We have never had the illusion that peace and freedom could be based on weakness.

—Franklin D. Roosevelt, address on the one hundredth
anniversary of the Virginia Military Institute,
Lexington, Virginia, November 11, 1939

❧

After the first World War we tried to achieve a formula for permanent peace, based on a magnificent idealism. We failed. But, by our failure, we have learned that we cannot maintain peace at this stage of human development by good intentions alone. Today the United Nations are the mightiest military coalition in history. They represent an overwhelming majority of the population of the world. Bound together in solemn agreement that they themselves will not commit acts of aggression or conquest against any of their neighbors, the United Nations can and must remain united for the maintenance of peace by preventing any attempt to rearm in Germany, in Japan, in Italy, or in any other nation which seeks to violate the Tenth Commandment—"Thou shalt not covet."

—Franklin D. Roosevelt, State of the Union address,
January 7, 1943

Peace, like charity, begins at home.

> —Franklin D. Roosevelt, speech in Chatauqua,
> New York, August 14, 1936

❧

If the human race as a whole is to survive, the world must find the way by which men and nations can live together in peace. We cannot accept the doctrine that war must be forever a part of man's destiny.

> —Franklin D. Roosevelt, campaign address in
> Cleveland, November 2, 1940

❧

We seek peace—enduring peace. More than an end to war, we want an end to the beginnings of all wars—yes, an end to this brutal, inhuman, and thoroughly impractical method of settling the differences between governments.

> —Franklin D. Roosevelt, undelivered address
> prepared for Jefferson Day, April 13, 1945

❧

We have to face the fact that either all of us are going to die together or we are going to learn to live together and if we are to live together we have to talk.

> —Eleanor Roosevelt, quoted in *The New York Times*,
> October 15, 1960

For it isn't enough to talk about peace. One must believe in it. And it isn't enough to believe in it. One must work at it.

—Eleanor Roosevelt, radio broadcast, Voice of America,
November 11, 1951

❧

War is a contagion.

—Franklin D. Roosevelt, speech, Chicago, October 5, 1937

❧

Battles are not won by soldiers or sailors who think first of their own personal safety. And wars are not won by people who are concerned primarily with their own comfort, their own convenience, their own pocketbooks.

—Franklin D. Roosevelt, Labor Day radio address,
September 7, 1942

❧

I have seen war. I have seen war on land and sea. I have seen blood running from the wounded. I have seen men coughing out their gassed lungs. I have seen the dead in the mud. I have seen cities destroyed. I have seen two hundred limping, exhausted men come out of line—the survivors of a regiment of one thousand that went forward forty-eight hours before. I have seen children starving. I have seen the agony of mothers and wives. I hate war.

—Franklin D. Roosevelt, speech in Chautauqua,
New York, August 14, 1936

Every right-thinking man and woman in our country wishes that it were safe for the nation to spend less of our national budget on our armed forces. All know that we are faced with a condition and not a theory—and that the condition is not of our choosing.

—Franklin D. Roosevelt, address on national defense,
San Francisco, July 14, 1938

෴

We, at home, owe a special and continuing obligation to these men and women in the armed services. During the war we have seen to it that they have received the best training and equipment, the best food, shelter, and medical attention, the best protection and care which planning, ingenuity, physical resources, and money could furnish in time of war. But after the war shall have been won, the best way that we can repay a portion of that debt is to see to it, by planning and by action now, that those men and women are demobilized into an economy which is sound and prosperous, with a minimum of unemployment and dislocation; and that, with the assistance of government, they are given the opportunity to find a job for which they are fitted and trained, in a field which offers some reasonable assurance of well-being and continuous employment.

—Franklin D. Roosevelt, message to Congress on educational opportunities
for war veterans, October 27, 1943

෴

Life in the armed services is hard and uncomfortable, but I think women can stand up under that type of living just as well as men.

—Eleanor Roosevelt, "My Day," October 15, 1943

It is not a sacrifice for any man, old or young, to be in the Army or the Navy of the United States. Rather, it is a privilege.

—Franklin D. Roosevelt, radio address delivered two days after the attack on Pearl Harbor, December 9, 1941

The motto of war is: "Let the strong survive; let the weak die." The motto of peace is: "Let the strong help the weak to survive."

—Franklin D. Roosevelt, speech before the Congress and Supreme Court of Brazil, Rio de Janeiro, Brazil, November 27, 1936

In the field of world policy I would dedicate this Nation to the policy of the good neighbor—the neighbor who resolutely respects himself and, because he does so, respects the rights of others—the neighbor who respects his obligations and respects the sanctity of his agreements in and with a world of neighbors.

—Franklin D. Roosevelt, first inaugural address, March 4, 1933

We must keep the faith, strive to strengthen the U.N. which is the one machine through which we must work for greater understanding and eventually, we hope, for a peaceful world.

—Eleanor Roosevelt, *Meriden Daily Journal*, July 23, 1952

I think that if the atomic bomb did nothing more, it scared the people to the point where they realized that either they must do something about preventing war or there is a chance that there might be a morning when we would not wake up.

—Eleanor Roosevelt, press conference,
January 3, 1946

I think it is nonsense to build bomb shelters. It is quite evident, from all we are told about modern nuclear weapons, that the shelters would be useless. We had better bend our efforts to preventing nuclear war and not worry about how we can preserve our own skins. I do not approve of individuals' building shelters, and I would consider it a waste of government money to build them for public use.

—Eleanor Roosevelt, "If You Ask Me," *McCall's*, November 1960

The work, my friends, is peace. More than an end of this war—an end to the beginnings of all wars. Yes, an end, forever, to this impractical, unrealistic settlement of the differences between governments by the mass killing of peoples.

—Franklin D. Roosevelt, undelivered address
prepared for Jefferson Day, April 13, 1945

LOVE, MARRIAGE, FAMILY, AND FRIENDS

He was young and gay and good-looking and I was shy and awkward and thrilled when he asked me to dance.

> —Eleanor Roosevelt, recalling an encounter with
> Franklin when she was a young teenager

∾

I solemnly answered "yes," and yet I know now that it was years later before I understood what being in love or what loving really meant.

> —Eleanor Roosevelt recalling her answer to her grandmother,
> who inquired if she was really in love with Franklin
> after learning of their engagement

∾

I know what pain I must have caused you and you know I wouldn't do it if I really could have helped it. . . . I know my mind, have known it for a long time, and know that I could never think otherwise: Result: I am the happiest man just now in the world; likewise the luckiest—And for you, dear Mummy, you know that nothing can ever change what we have always been & always will be to each other—only now you have two children to love & to love you—and Eleanor as you know will always be a daughter to you in every true way.

> —Franklin D. Roosevelt's letter to his mother after
> informing her of his intention to marry Eleanor,
> November 1903

I love you dearest and I hope that I shall always prove worthy of the love which you have given me. I have never known before what it was to be absolutely happy nor have I ever longed for just one glimpse of a pair of eyes.

—Eleanor Roosevelt, letter to Franklin during their engagement, 1903

We are full of health and bursting with food (at least I am) and the only unkind word Eleanor has ever said to me is that she would like to see me bust!

—Franklin Roosevelt's letter to his mother
from his European honeymoon, 1905

Kiss the chicks and take very good care of yourself, dearest. . . . I long so to be with you and this bachelor life isn't what it's cracked up to be.

—Franklin D. Roosevelt, letter to Eleanor while he was working in
Washington (as assistant secretary of the Navy) and she and the
children summered at their home on Campobello Island, 1916

Keeping up romance, keeping up constant interest in each other by meticulous care for the little things which were important when you were in love, this is all a part of loving.

—Eleanor Roosevelt, "My Day," October 20, 1939

It is obviously true that the first flush of being "in love" always changes into something deeper and calmer, or more superficial. I have known only a few very happy marriages. By that I do not mean just people who get along together and live contentedly through life, but people who are really excitingly happy.

—Eleanor Roosevelt, "My Day," February 8, 1944

❧

There is no more precious experience in life than friendship. And I am not forgetting love and marriage as I write this; the lovers, or the man and wife, who are not friends are but weakly joined together.

—Eleanor Roosevelt, *Eleanor Roosevelt's Book of Common Sense Etiquette*, 1962

❧

Friendship with oneself is all-important, because without it one cannot be friends with anyone else in the world.

—Eleanor Roosevelt, "How to Take Criticism," *Ladies Home Journal*, November 1944

❧

Marriages and the upbringing of children in the home require as well trained a mind and as well-disciplined a character as any other occupation that might be considered a career.

—Eleanor Roosevelt, "My Day," March 29, 1941

I think people are happier in marriage when neither one is the boss, but when both of them are willing to give as well as take.

—Eleanor Roosevelt, "If You Ask Me," *Ladies Home Journal*, September 1944

I think, at a child's birth, if a mother could ask a fairy godmother to endow it with the most useful gift, that gift would be curiosity.

—Eleanor Roosevelt, quoted in *Today's Health*, October 1966

The most important thing for a child is to acquire an attitude of responsibility. School is his job, and he should consider it as such.

—Eleanor Roosevelt, *The New York Times Magazine*, December 4, 1932

As parents, we must realize that modern life tends to make us soft, and we must let our children meet their own difficulties, find their own solutions to knotty problems and gain experience in themselves.

—Eleanor Roosevelt, *Parent's Magazine*, June 1931

We may not be able to prepare the future for our children, but we can at least prepare our children for the future.

—Franklin D. Roosevelt

I was so concerned with bringing up my children properly that I was not wise enough to love them. Now, looking back, I think I would rather spoil a child a little and have more fun out of it.

—Eleanor Roosevelt, *The Autobiography of Eleanor Roosevelt*, 1961

❦

Of course the thing that I am proudest of is that I have produced five children, all of whom, I can say without reservation, are pretty nice people.

—Eleanor Roosevelt, *The New York Times*, October 8, 1944

❦

I had a feeling that I might be saying good-bye for the last time. It was sort of a precursor of what it would be like if your children were killed and never to come back. Life had to go on and you had to do what was required of you, but something inside you quietly died.

—Eleanor Roosevelt, about parting with her sons as they left for the war, *This I Remember*, 1949

❦

We all of us owe, I imagine, far more than we realize to our friends as well as to the members of our family. I know that in my own case my friends are responsible for much that I have become and without them there are many things which would have remained closed books to me.

—Eleanor Roosevelt, *The Autobiography of Eleanor Roosevelt*, 1961

After the party for the staff in the East Room, the little children had their supper while the big children decorated the family tree on the second floor. My husband would often start to read *A Christmas Carol* and would finish after dinner. Later in the evening, I always filled the Christmas stockings, which were hung in my husband's bedroom, and then attended church services, beginning at eleven-thirty. Getting to bed was a late affair, for every stocking had to be replaced exactly where each child or grandchild had hung it up.

> —Eleanor Roosevelt, recalling Christmas during the White House years, "If You Ask Me," *McCall's*, December 1959

A woman, just like a man, may have a great gift for some particular thing. That does not mean that she must give up the joy of marrying and having a home and children.

> —Eleanor Roosevelt, *It's Up to the Women*, 1933

I learned something which has stood me in good stead many times—the most important thing in any relationship is not what you get but what you give.

> —Eleanor Roosevelt, *The Autobiography of Eleanor Roosevelt*, 1961

LIFE'S PLEASURES

His stamps were his best-known collection, well over a million of them in 150 matching albums. His physician . . . who saw him nearly every day in the White House, estimated that FDR spent at least 2,140 hours poring over these bright bits of paper during his dozen busy years in the White House.

—Geoffrey C. Ward, *Before the Trumpet: Young Franklin Roosevelt 1882–1905*, 1985

❧

One thing life has taught me: if you are interested, you never have to look for new interests. They come to you. . . . All you need to do is to be curious, receptive, eager for experience. And there's one strange thing: when you are genuinely interested in one thing, it will always lead to something else.

—Eleanor Roosevelt, *You Learn by Living*, 1960

❧

One of the blessings of life in the rural areas is the fact that any child or adult can escape and be alone with nature at a moment's notice.

—Eleanor Roosevelt, "My Day," June 28, 1944

❧

Art is not a treasure in the past or an importation from another land, but part of the present life of all the living and creating peoples.

—Franklin D. Roosevelt, dedication address, National Gallery of Art, 1941

I think poetry read aloud is one of the great pleasures which companionable people may enjoy together.

—Eleanor Roosevelt, "My Day," July 6, 1945

∾

I'm the kind of fan who wants to get plenty of action for my money. I get the biggest kick out of the biggest score—a game in which the hitters pole the ball into the far corners of the field, the outfielders scramble and men run the bases.

—Franklin D. Roosevelt on baseball

∾

I honestly feel that it would be best for the country to keep baseball going. There will be fewer people unemployed and everybody will work longer hours and harder than ever before. And that means that they ought to have a chance for recreation and for taking their minds off their work even more than before. Baseball provides a recreation which does not last over two hours or two hours and a half, and which can be got for very little cost. And, incidentally, I hope that night games can be extended because it gives an opportunity to the day shift to see a game occasionally.

—Franklin D. Roosevelt, letter to Commissioner Landis
advocating the continuation of professional baseball
during the war, January 15, 1942

No amount of TV watching will give you the satisfaction that
comes from being able to read and re-read a book you have enjoyed.

—Eleanor Roosevelt, "My Day,"
April 17, 1961

The President has warned that we are becoming a nation of
spectators rather than partakers. If our added leisure means watching
baseball and football on television, with no real occupation in which
we put our own brains and energies to work, then I must join the
President in his exhortation to begin to do things, not just watch
things being done.

—Eleanor Roosevelt, "My Day,"
November 5, 1958

I think the main rule to follow is always to be kind and thoughtful
to everybody with whom you come in contact; to show your
gratitude for little things; to learn, before you go, some of the
customs and habits of the countries you visit, so as not to offend
inadvertently. Be interested in what you see, and don't always be
comparing things unfavorably with what you have at home.

—Eleanor Roosevelt, in response to a question about how
Americans might behave while traveling abroad,
"If You Ask Me," *McCall's*, February 1961

HISTORY AND RELIGION

All big changes in human history have been arrived at slowly and through many compromises.

—Eleanor Roosevelt, 1925

∿

There is no question in my mind that it is time for the country to become fairly radical for a generation. History shows that where this occurs occasionally, nations are saved from revolution.

—Franklin D. Roosevelt, letter to John A. Kingsbury, May 1930

∿

History proves that dictatorships do not grow out of strong and successful governments, but out of weak and helpless ones. If by democratic methods people get a government strong enough to protect them from fear and starvation, their democracy succeeds; but if they do not, they grow impatient. Therefore, the only sure bulwark of continuing liberty is a government strong enough to protect the interests of the people, and a people strong enough and well enough informed to maintain its sovereign control over its government.

—Franklin D. Roosevelt, radio address, April 14, 1938

∿

History is filled with unforeseeable situations that call for some flexibility of action.

—Franklin D. Roosevelt, statement on neutrality legislation,
August 31, 1935

The value of history lies almost entirely in the insight which it gives to us as to what things in civilization have really had enduring value.

—Eleanor Roosevelt, "My Day," July 31, 1943

∾

One thing I believe profoundly: We make our own history. The course of history is directed by the choices we make and our choices grow out of the ideas, the beliefs, the values, the dreams of the people. It is not so much the powerful leaders that determine our destiny as the much more powerful influence of the combined voices of the people themselves.

—Eleanor Roosevelt, *Tomorrow Is Now*, 1963

∾

If we have learned anything from history it is that vindictiveness does not lead to greater happiness, either to the victim or the conqueror.

—Eleanor Roosevelt, White House press conference, February 7, 1939

∾

All of recorded history bears witness that the human race has made true advancement only as it has appreciated spiritual values. Those unhappy peoples who have placed their sole reliance on the sword have inevitably perished by the sword in the end. Physical force can never permanently withstand the impact of spiritual force.

—Franklin D. Roosevelt, address at the dedication of Woodrow Wilson's birthplace, Staunton, Virginia, May 4, 1941

Religion, by teaching man his relationship to God, gives the individual a sense of his own dignity and teaches him to respect himself by respecting his neighbors.

—Franklin D. Roosevelt, State of the Union address, January 4, 1939

❧

In the whole history of mankind, far back into the dim past before man knew how to record thoughts or events, the human race has been distinguished from other forms of life by the existence, the fact, of religion. Periodic attempts to deny God have always come and will always come to naught.

—Franklin D. Roosevelt, address before the Inter-American Conference for the Maintenance of Peace in Buenos Aires, Argentina, December 1, 1936

❧

We are a mixed nation of many peoples and many religions, but most of us would accept the life of Christ as a pattern for our democratic way of life, and Christ taught love and never hate.

—Eleanor Roosevelt, "My Day," July 14, 1943

❧

I doubt if there is in the world a single problem, whether social, political, or economic, which would not find ready solution if men and nations would rule their lives according to the plain teaching of the Sermon on the Mount.

—Franklin D. Roosevelt, April 15, 1938

Religion in wide areas of the earth is being confronted with irreligion; our faiths are being challenged. It is because of that threat that you and I must reach across the lines between our creeds, clasp hands, and make common cause.

—Franklin D. Roosevelt, radio address on Brotherhood Day,
February 23, 1936

∾

I doubt that anyone does not really believe in God. People may think they don't have any belief, but you will usually find that there is a belief in something beyond himself. In any case, I would not judge a man's character by his belief or unbelief. I would judge his character by his deeds; and no matter what he said about his beliefs, his behavior would soon show whether he was a man of good character or bad.

—Eleanor Roosevelt, *The Wisdom of Eleanor Roosevelt*, 1963

∾

The important thing is neither your nationality nor the religion you professed, but how your faith translated itself in your life.

—Eleanor Roosevelt, "My Day," September 16, 1943

WIT AND WISDOM

If you treat people right they will treat you right—ninety percent of the time.

—Franklin D. Roosevelt

There is nothing I love so much as a good fight.

—Franklin D. Roosevelt, interview in *The New York Times*, January 22, 1911

Judge me by the enemies I've made.

—Franklin D. Roosevelt

I am a Christian and a Democrat—that's all.

—Franklin D. Roosevelt in response to a reporter's question about his political philosophy

If we can "boondoggle" ourselves out of this depression, that word is going to be enshrined in the hearts of the American people for years to come.

—Franklin D. Roosevelt, speech to the New Jersey State Emergency Council in Newark, New Jersey, January 18, 1936

Once you've spent two years trying to wiggle one toe, everything is in proportion.

—Franklin D. Roosevelt

I am very much in favor of the kind of war that we are conducting here at Warm Springs, the kind of war that, aided and abetted by what we have been doing at Warm Springs now for fourteen or fifteen years, is spreading all over the country—the war against the crippling of men and women and, especially, of children.

—Franklin D. Roosevelt, remarks at Thanksgiving Day dinner, Warm Springs, Georgia, November 23, 1939

Competition has been shown to be useful up to a certain point and no further, but cooperation, which is the thing we must strive for today, begins where competition leaves off.

—Franklin D. Roosevelt, speech at the People's Forum in Troy, New York, March 3, 1912

To accomplish almost anything worthwhile, it is necessary to compromise between the ideal and the practical.

—Franklin D. Roosevelt, quoted in "How the President Works," *Harper's*, June 1936

When you get to the end of your rope, tie a knot and hang on.

—Franklin D. Roosevelt

❧

You sometimes find something good in the lunatic fringe. In fact, we have got as part of our social and economic government today a whole lot of things which in my boyhood were considered lunatic fringe, and yet they are now part of everyday life.

—Franklin D. Roosevelt, press conference, May 30, 1944

❧

You gain strength, courage, and confidence by every experience in which you really stop to look fear in the face.

—Eleanor Roosevelt, *You Learn by Living*, 1960

❧

My greatest fear has always been that I would be afraid—afraid physically or mentally or morally and allow myself to be influenced by fear instead of by my honest convictions.

—Eleanor Roosevelt, *If You Ask Me*, 1946

❧

No one can make you feel inferior without your consent.

—Eleanor Roosevelt

As for accomplishments, I just did what I had to do as things came along.

—Eleanor Roosevelt, quoted in *The New York Times*, October 8, 1954

❧

A mature person is one who does not think only in absolutes, who is able to be objective even when deeply stirred emotionally, who has learned that there is both good and bad in all people and in all things, and who walks humbly and deals charitably with the circumstances of life, knowing that in this world no one is all-knowing and therefore all of us need both love and charity.

—Eleanor Roosevelt, *It Seems to Me*, 1954

❧

Courage is more exhilarating than fear and in the long run it is easier. We do not have to become heroes overnight. Just a step at a time, meeting each thing that comes up, seeing it is not as dreadful as it appeared, discovering we have the strength to stare it down.

—Eleanor Roosevelt, *You Learn by Living*, 1960

❧

There is a longing in the air. It is not a longing to go back to what they call "the good old days." I have distinct reservations as to how good "the good old days" were. I would rather believe that we can achieve new and better days.

—Franklin D. Roosevelt, address before the Canadian Parliament, Ottawa, August 25, 1943

I could not, at any age, be content to take my place in a corner by the fireside and simply look on. Life was meant to be lived. Curiosity must be kept alive. The fatal thing is the rejection. One must never, for whatever reason, turn his back on life.

—Eleanor Roosevelt, *The Autobiography of Eleanor Roosevelt*, 1961

No, I have never wanted to be a man. I have often wanted to be more effective as a woman, but I have never felt that trousers would do the trick!

—Eleanor Roosevelt, *If You Ask Me*, 1946

One of the blessings of age is to learn not to part on a note of sharpness, to treasure the moments spent with those we love, and to make them whenever possible good to remember, for time is short.

—Eleanor Roosevelt, "My Day," February 5, 1943

Surely, in the light of history, it is more intelligent to hope rather than to fear, to try rather than not to try. For one thing we know beyond all doubt: Nothing has ever been achieved by the person who says, "It can't be done."

—Eleanor Roosevelt, *You Learn By Living*, 1960

You must do the thing you think you cannot do.

—Eleanor Roosevelt, *You Learn by Living*, 1960

❧

I do not look upon these United States as a finished product. We are still in the making.

—Franklin D. Roosevelt, radio address on Brotherhood Day, 1936

❧

We have always held to the hope, the belief, the conviction, that there is a better life, a better world, beyond the horizon.

—Franklin D. Roosevelt, address in Dayton, Ohio, October 12, 1940

❧

Human kindness has never weakened the stamina or softened the fiber of a free people. A nation does not have to be cruel to be tough.

—Franklin D. Roosevelt, speech, 1935

❧

The only limit to our realization of tomorrow will be our doubts of today. Let us move forward with strong and active faith.

—Franklin D. Roosevelt, undelivered address prepared for Jefferson Day, April 13, 1945

REMEMBERING
FRANKLIN AND ELEANOR

Do you realize that you are approaching manhood and next year, when you begin your university life, you will be away from the safeguards of school and will have to withstand many temptations? . . . But I always feel your character is so well formed and established I have no fear.

—James Roosevelt's letter to Franklin on his
seventeenth birthday, June 30, 1899

∼

Part of the attraction between Eleanor and Franklin Roosevelt was their noble aspirations. Part was desire for a different life from what they had known growing up. . . . The Roosevelts both had firm goals in life and already were showing signs of the qualities of intelligence and leadership that would make some of the goals attainable.

—Frank Freidel, *Franklin D. Roosevelt:
A Rendezvous with Destiny*, 1990

∼

We are greatly rejoiced over the good news. I am as fond of Eleanor as if she were my daughter; and I like you, and trust you, and believe in you. No other success in life—not the Presidency, or anything else—begins to compare with the joy and happiness that come in and from the love of the true man and the true woman. . . . You and Eleanor are true and brave, and I believe you love each other unselfishly; and golden years open before you. May all good fortune attend you both, ever.

—Letter from Theodore Roosevelt to Franklin
about the pending marriage, November 1904

He took us on many weekends down the Potomac, and we would go hiking, looking up old houses, these big old Southern homes, some of which were falling down. . . . We did a great deal of sightseeing and listening to his stories of the history of the country down in Virginia. . . . Father stands out because he was so active and he led the way.

—Anna Roosevelt Halsted

Franklin did not like to administer discipline. As public responsibilities more and more cut down the time he was able to spend with his "chicks," he wanted the hours he was with them to be full of fun, excitement, and affection. His mother had always tried to run him, and he shied away from doing the same to his children. He was loath to hurt anyone's feelings, and preferred to be the agent of good tidings.

—Joseph P. Lash, *Eleanor and Franklin*, 1971

Franklin's illness . . . gave him strength and courage he had not had before. He had to think out the fundamentals of living and learn the greatest of all lessons—infinite patience and never ending persistence.

—Eleanor Roosevelt, inscription from the Franklin Delano Roosevelt Memorial, Washington, D.C.

Terrible as it was for him, he had the mental depth and the compassion to realize how overwhelmingly frightening it was for his children, and he tried to lighten our fears.

—James Roosevelt, recalling his father's diagnosis of polio

The greatest thing he accomplished was to make people all over the world feel that he, and therefore our country, actually was concerned about them and was interested in their problems.

—Eleanor Roosevelt, quoted in the *News and Courier*, April 10, 1955

As for being crippled, [Father] disregarded that completely, driving from his mind any thought that he was less than a normal man. Taking risks was a compulsion, to prove to himself that he was no invalid.

—Elliott Roosevelt, *A Rendezvous with Destiny: The Roosevelts of the White House* by Elliott Roosevelt and James Brough, 1975

What Papa really liked to do for relaxation was work on his stamp collection. . . . He'd invite me over and explain what he was doing, showing me a stamp from some exotic place, such as Samoa, and I'd then get a brief geography lesson—until my mother came in and, finding me interrupting him, led me away.

—Curtis Roosevelt, *Too Close to the Sun: Growing Up in the Shadow of My Grandparents, Franklin and Eleanor*, 2008

May I say the greatest boon which has come to me in this life was my friendship with this great man, whose interest in the "forgotten man" was not an empty gesture but the very obsession of his heart and life.

—Judge Henry Revill, quoted in the *Rome News-Tribune*, April 12, 1955

∿

If anything happened to that man, I couldn't stand it. He is the truest friend; he has the farthest vision; he is the greatest man I have ever known.

—Winston Churchill to American Vice Consul Kenneth Pendar
at the Casablanca Conference, June 1943

∿

They looked like two little boys playing soldier. They seemed to be having a wonderful time, too wonderful in fact. It made me a little sad somehow.

—Eleanor Roosevelt about Franklin and Winston Churchill, having
observed them strategizing in the White House map room
after the attack on Pearl Harbor in December 1941

∿

He was the first chief executive to fly, to leave the country in wartime, to report to the people by radio, to place a woman in the Cabinet, to write directly to the emperor of Japan—just because nobody ever had done it before.

—Douglas B. Cornell, *News and Courier*, April 10, 1955

Meeting Franklin Roosevelt was like opening your first bottle of champagne; knowing him was like drinking it.

—**Winston Churchill**

❧

There seemed to be real friendship & understanding between F.D.R. & Churchill. . . . F.D.R.'s manner was easy and intimate—His face humorous, or very serious, according to the subject of conversation, and entirely natural. Not a trace of having to guard his words or expressions, just the opposite of his manner at a press conference, when he is an actor on a stage—and a player on an instrument, at the same time.

—**Daisy Suckley, FDR's distant cousin and friend, on seeing FDR and Churchill meet for the first time**

❧

I lay in my berth all night, with the window shade up, looking out at the countryside Franklin had loved. I was truly surprised by the people along the way. I had never realized the full scope of their devotion to him until he died.

—**Eleanor Roosevelt, recalling the train trip in which FDR's body was brought back to Washington D.C., April 1945**

❧

Many people tell me that my husband's voice in their homes actually made them feel that they were part of his family.

—**Eleanor Roosevelt, "My Day," May 12, 1945**

He did his job to the end as he would want you to do. Bless you all and all our love. Mother.

—Eleanor Roosevelt's cable to her four sons, all on active military service, upon FDR's death

❧

No matter when this man might have left us, we would have felt that we had suffered an irreplaceable loss . . . .

—Albert Einstein, statement on Roosevelt's death, April 27, 1945

❧

The New Deal made possible the great postwar housing boom that populated the Sun Belt and boosted millions of Americans into the middle class, where, ironically, they often became Republicans.

—Jonathan Alter, *The Defining Moment: FDR's Hundred Days and the Triumph of Hope*, 2006

❧

The Depression gave F.D.R. the chance to use the power of government to complete the work his cousin had begun: to build a great middle class, help the poor work their way into it and give Americans a modicum of security in old age. His leadership during World War II and the plans he made for the U.N. and a permanent leadership role for the U.S. on the world stage cemented his legacy as one of our greatest Presidents.

—Bill Clinton, *Time Magazine*, "The Legacy of FDR: Getting It Right," July 2009

I think F.D.R. was very much attracted to my grandmother because they were two lonely people, two people who were not totally satisfied with the standards and ideals of their upper-class group. And I think the two of them looked at each other and knew that they could draw strength from each other.

—Curtis Roosevelt, grandson of Franklin and Eleanor Roosevelt

&

Franklin, a strong, stubborn, secretive person, met his match in Eleanor, equally strong and stubborn but forthright. For all their high ideals they were to have difficulty in communicating with each other, especially concerning Franklin's mother.

—Frank Freidel, *Franklin D. Roosevelt: A Rendezvous with Destiny*, 1990

&

My grandmother was charming, gracious, and always sincerely concerned, yet understanding how to entertain a three-year-old and a six-year-old—how to enter their world and enjoy their pleasures—didn't come as easily to her as it did to Papa. There remained a reserve within her—even when she obviously cared for and loved someone—that kept her from ever releasing herself totally with another human being. It was a wall that was always there.

—Curtis Roosevelt, *Too Close to the Sun: Growing Up in the Shadow of My Grandparents, Franklin and Eleanor*, 2008

Her genius is the capacity to love the human race and to hear and understand the misery and wants and aspirations of the people.

—Frances Perkins, United States secretary of labor during Roosevelt administration, quoted in *The New York Times*, June 25, 1936

∾

She shattered the ceremonial mold in which the role of the first lady had traditionally been fashioned, and reshaped it around her own skills and commitments to social reform.

—Doris Kearns Goodwin, *No Ordinary Time: Franklin and Eleanor Roosevelt: The Home Front in World War II*, 1994

∾

Like so many others, I have lost more than a beloved friend. I have lost an inspiration. She would rather light a candle than curse the darkness, and her glow has warmed the world.

—Adlai Stevenson, eulogy for Eleanor Roosevelt in the United Nations General Assembly, November 7, 1962

CHRONOLOGY OF FRANKLIN AND ELEANOR ROOSEVELT

JANUARY 30, 1882 — Franklin Delano Roosevelt is born in Hyde Park, New York.

OCTOBER 11, 1884 — Anna Eleanor Roosevelt is born in New York City.

1896 TO 1900 — FDR is homeschooled until 1896 when he is sent to Groton, a private preparatory school in Massachusetts.

1899 — Eleanor attends Allenswood School in England for three years. In 1902 she returns to New York City and makes her society debut at the Waldorf-Astoria.

1900 TO 1903 — FDR attends Harvard and receives a BA in history.

MARCH 17, 1905 — After a yearlong secret engagement, FDR marries his fifth cousin, once removed, Eleanor Roosevelt, in New York City. President Theodore Roosevelt, Eleanor's uncle, walks her down the aisle. FDR enters Columbia Law School.

1906 — ER gives birth to their first child, Anna.

1907 — ER gives birth to their second child, James. FDR passes the bar exam and leaves Columbia before completing his law degree.

1909 — ER gives birth to their third child, Franklin Jr. He dies during infancy from influenza.

1910 — ER gives birth to their fourth child, Elliott. FDR is elected to the New York State Senate and the family moves to Albany.

1913 — FDR is appointed assistant secretary of the United States Navy by President Woodrow Wilson. The family moves to Washington, D.C.

JULY 28, 1914 — World War I erupts in Europe. In August, ER gives birth to their fifth child, who is also named Franklin Jr.

1916 — ER gives birth to their sixth child, John.

APRIL 6, 1917— The United States enters World War I.

1918 — ER discovers FDR is having an affair with her social secretary, Lucy Mercer. ER volunteers for the Red Cross, United States Navy, and Navy League to help World War I veterans. She also attends the Paris Peace Conference.

1920 — FDR runs for vice president on Democratic ticket with James Cox of Ohio; ER campaigns with him. Election is lost to Warren Harding. FDR returns to private life. Congress passes the nineteenth amendment giving women the right to vote.

1921— FDR contracts polio and is paralyzed. ER nurses him and encourages him to return to politics.

1925 — FDR builds Val-Kill Estate for ER in Hyde Park; she founds the Val-Kill furniture factory with friends Marion Dickerman and Nancy Cook. The following year, the three women purchase Todhunter School, a girls seminary in New York where ER teaches history and government.

1928 — FDR is elected governor of New York State.

1932 — FDR is nominated as Democratic Party candidate and defeats Hoover in presidential election by seven million votes.

1933 — FDR implements the New Deal—a sweeping legislative initiative to affect economic relief, recovery, and reform. ER becomes the first-ever first lady to hold all-female press conferences. She advocates for the coal miners of West Virginia and publishes *It's Up to the Women*.

1935 — Further New Deal legislation is enacted, such as the Works Progress Administration and Social Security. ER begins publishing her syndicated column "My Day," which she continues for the rest of her life.

1936 — FDR is reelected president for a second term.

1937 — To combat the Supreme Court's efforts to thwart his New Deal legislation, FDR proposes judicial reforms that would add additional justices to the Supreme Court. The plan fails but the Supreme Court starts ruling more in favor of New Deal legislation. ER's book *This Is My Story* is published. The following year, she writes *This Troubled World*.

1939 — ER resigns her membership from the Daughters of the American Revolution in protest of Marian Anderson's exclusion from Constitution Hall. She arranges for Anderson to sing at the Lincoln Memorial on Easter Sunday and 75,000 people attend. World War II breaks out in Europe after Hitler invades Poland.

1940 — FDR is reelected president for a third term.

1941 — FDR signs Lend-Lease bill in March to aid Allied forces. ER begins writing syndicated column "If You Ask Me."

DECEMBER 7, 1941 — Japan bombs Pearl Harbor and the United States enters World War II.

1942 — FDR initiates building of "grand alliance" of Allied nations through the formation of the United Nations. ER flies with the Tuskegee Airmen.

1944 — FDR is reelected president for a fourth term.

1945 — FDR, Churchill, and Stalin meet at Yalta. ER encourages the Army Nurses Corp to include African-American women as members. She also joins the NAACP board of directors.

APRIL 12, 1945 — FDR dies in Warm Springs, Georgia. He is buried in the Rose Garden at Hyde Park, New York.

1946 — ER refuses congressional pension. She is appointed United States delegate to the United Nations and is elected head of the United Nations Human Rights Commission. She begins drafting the Declaration of Human Rights.

1947 — ER advocates for a separate Jewish state.

1948 — The Human Rights Declaration is passed by the United Nations.

1949 — ER writes *This I Remember*.

1951 — ER and her son Elliott host NBC television and radio shows with guests such as Albert Einstein.

1952 — ER campaigns for Adlai Stevenson; she resigns from the United Nations after Dwight Eisenhower wins the presidential election.

1953 — ER writes *India and the Awakening East* and *UN Today and Tomorrow* (with William DeWitt). The following year, she writes *Ladies of Courage* with friend Lorena Hickock and *It Seems to Me*.

1957 — ER visits Soviet Union and meets with Nikita Khrushchev.

1958 — ER writes *On My Own*. She speaks at a civil rights event in Tennessee despite threats from the Ku Klux Klan.

1960 — ER campaigns for JFK. She writes *You Learn by Living*.

1961— ER writes *The Autobiography of Eleanor Roosevelt*. JFK reappoints ER to the United Nations as chair of the President's Commission on the Status of Women.

NOVEMBER 7, 1962 — ER dies in New York City from tuberculosis and is buried in the Rose Garden next to FDR at Hyde Park on November 10th.